I DEDICATE THIS BOOK TO MY FIVE BEAUTIFUL CHILDREN ELENA, ALEXA, SIENNA, NOAH, AND BRYNA.

MAY YOU FIND AMONG THESE PAGES A SPARK OF WONDER AND JOY THAT LIGHTS UP YOUR HEARTS EVERYDAY. I PRAY YOU ALLOW THIS BOOK TO REMIND YOU THAT YOU ARE SURROUNDED BY A CIRCLE OF LOVE AND PROTECTION.

YOUR ANGELS, JUST LIKE ME, ARE ALWAYS WITH YOU -- GUIDING, COMFORTING, PROTECTING, AND CHEERING YOU ON. AS YOU JOURNEY THROUGH LIFE'S ADVENTURES, KNOW THAT YOU ARE NEVER ALONE.

WITH ALL MY LOVE,
MOM:)

AS I LAY IN BED AT NIGHT, I ASK FOR ANGELS TO BE MY LIGHT.

AND I KNOW THEY WILL TAKE AWAY ALL OF MY FEAR.

I SEE ANGEL WARRIORS INSTEAD.

AND WHEN THERE IS DARKNESS THEIR LIGHT BEAMS.

AND PICTURE THEM WITH ME IN EVERY WAY.

AND THEY PUT ON THEIR SUPERHERO MASK.

TO THINGS AS LIGHT AS A FEATHER.

AND TRUST THEY WILL HELP MAKE ALL MY DREAMS APPEAR.